ANTONOV AN-225 MRIYA

BY QUINN M. ARNOLD

CREATIVE EDUCATION • CREATIVE PAPERBACKS

Published by Creative Education and Creative Paperbacks
P.O. Box 227, Mankato, Minnesota 56002
Creative Education and Creative Paperbacks are imprints
of The Creative Company
www.thecreativecompany.us

Design by The Design Lab
Production by Chelsey Luther
Art direction by Rita Marshall
Printed in the United States of America

Photographs by Alamy (Chris Alan Wilton), Corbis (Reuters,
Marin Tomaš/Demotix), Getty Images (Bloomberg, SVF2),
Shutterstock (Davide Calabresi, InsectWorld, OPIS Zagreb)

Library of Congress Cataloging-in-Publication Data
Arnold, Quinn M.
Antonov An-225 Mriya / by Quinn M. Arnold.
p. cm. — (Now that's big!)
Includes bibliographical references and index.
Summary: A high-interest introduction to the size, speed, and
purpose of the world's largest cargo plane, including a brief history
and what the future holds for the Antonov An-225.

ISBN 978-1-60818-711-9 (hardcover)
ISBN 978-1-62832-307-8 (pbk)
ISBN 978-1-5660-747-6 (eBook)
1. An-225 (Transport plane)—Juvenile literature. 2. Transport
planes—Juvenile literature.

UG1242.T7A76 2016
623.74/65—dc23   2015045203

CCSS: RI.1.1, 2, 3, 4, 5, 6, 7; RI.2.1, 2, 4, 5, 6, 7, 10; RF.1.1, 3, 4;
RF.2.3, 4

First Edition HC 9 8 7 6 5 4 3 2 1
First Edition PBK 9 8 7 6 5 4 3 2 1

TABLE OF CONTENTS

What plane is almost as long as a football field? The Antonov An-225 Mriya is the world's biggest cargo plane. It can move larger loads than any other plane.

5

The plane needs a two-mile-long (3.2 km) runway for takeoff.

The An-225 is as tall
as a six-story building.
Six powerful engines
help the plane fly. It
uses 32 wheels to land.

In 1988, the Soviet Union finished the only Mriya ever built. It was made to move the Soviet space shuttle. The An-225 flew with the shuttle on its back!

1988

It can take up to 12 hours to fuel the An-225.

The An-225 can go 528 miles (850 km) per hour. Most of the time it flies at 497 miles (800 km) per hour. It can hold 661,387 pounds (300,000 kg) of fuel. A fully loaded plane uses lots of gas. It has to stop often.

Mriya is a Ukrainian word that means "dream."

In 1994, people stopped using the An-225. Six years later, it was updated. Now countries all around the world use it.

1994

The nose opens up, and a ramp lowers to easily load cargo.

Cargo is loaded through the plane's nose. There is a lot of room. Eighty cars could fit inside. In 2001, the An-225 set a record for the heaviest flight. It held almost 280 tons (254 t) of cargo. That's heavier than 50 elephants!

Six city buses can fit inside the cargo hold!

The An-225 is a helpful plane because it can hold so much. It carries emergency aid to places after natural disasters. It has delivered machines, food, and supplies to Samoa, Japan, and other countries.

The Mriya's wingspan stretches 290 feet (88.4 m).

Someday, people will build an even bigger plane. But for now, the An-225 remains the giant of the sky.

HOW BIG

BLUE WHALE
100 ft (30.5 m)

ANTONOV AN-225 MRIYA
275.6 ft (84 m)

FIRST-GRADER
3.6 ft (1.1 m)

GIRAFFE
19 ft (5.8 m)

FEET

SEMITRAILER TRUCK
70 ft (21.3 m)

SPACE SHUTTLE
122 ft (37.2 m)

GLOSSARY

cargo plane—*an airplane that carries objects rather than people*

engines—*machines that use fuel to create movement*

natural disasters—*events such as earthquakes or storms that cause damage*

nose—*the front end of a plane*

space shuttle—*a spacecraft used to travel between Earth and space*

READ MORE

Bowman, Chris. *Monster Airplanes.*
Minneapolis: Bellwether Media, 2014.

Langley, Andrew. *Planes.*
Mankato, Minn.: Amicus, 2011.

WEBSITES

Idaho Public Television: Flight
http://idahoptv.org/sciencetrek/topics/flight/index.cfm
Click on the tabs to learn more about the history of flight, play games,
learn flight-related vocabulary, and more!

Paper Airplane Designs
http://www.foldnfly.com/#/1-1-1-1-1-1-1-1-2
Follow the instructions to build different types of paper airplanes.

Note: Every effort has been made to ensure that the websites listed above are suitable for children, that they have educational value, and that they contain no inappropriate material. However, because of the nature of the Internet, it is impossible to guarantee that these sites will remain active indefinitely or that their contents will not be altered.